THE JOURNAL OF JENS MUNK 1619–1620

The Journal
of Jens Munk
1619–1620

Edited and
with an Introduction
by W.A. Kenyon

ROM
Royal Ontario Museum
Toronto, Canada

© The Royal Ontario Museum, 1980
100 Queen's Park
Toronto, Ontario M5S 2C6

Canadian Cataloguing in Publication Data

Munk, Jens, 1579–1628.
  The journal of Jens Munk 1619–1620

ISBN 0-88854-264-X pa.

1. Munk, Jens, 1579–1628. 2. Northwest Passage.
3. Canada — Discovery and exploration — Danish.
4. Arctic regions — Danish exploration. I. Kenyon,
Walter A., 1917– II. Royal Ontario Museum.
III. Title.

FC3961.2.M85   910'.0916327   C80–094325–2
G650 1619 M85

Designed by Jean Lightfoot

Printed and bound in Canada by the Alger Press

Contents

Introduction

When Henry Hudson worked his way past Cape Wolstenholme in the summer of 1610, he saw an open sea stretching endlessly before him. It had been a hard passage, but a successful one, for Hudson believed that he had reached the fabled Pacific, that he had already sailed through the elusive northwest passage. But the men were restless, and the weather was bad in those high northern latitudes, so he shaped his course to the south. Following what he thought was the west coast of North America—or the back side of America, as it was called at the time—he hoped to reach a more congenial climate before heading west across the broad Pacific. Although we shall never know for sure, it is very likely that he would have headed for New Albion on the coast of California, where Francis Drake had careened the *Golden Hind* some thirty years earlier. But Hudson became trapped in a maze of shoals, reefs, and islands in what is now James Bay and was forced to winter there. The records of the wintering and the return voyage are extremely vague and sketchy because the crew mutinied, casting Hudson adrift in a small boat with eight of his men.

When Hudson's vessel, the fifty-five-ton *Discovery*, finally reached England, there were only eight survivors, led by Robert Bylot, who had formerly been Hudson's first mate. This half-starved band of mutineers would almost certainly have been hanged from the handiest yard-arm had it not been for one significant fact: mutineers they might be, but they were also the only men in the world who had ever sailed through the northwest passage. They alone knew the route to the Orient, the new route controlled by neither the Spaniards nor the Portuguese. Under the circumstances, they were just too valuable to be hanged. In fact, two of the survivors of the Hudson expedition, Robert Bylot and Abacuk Pricket, were sent off the following year with Thomas Button.

Button sailed from England in May 1612 with two ships—Hudson's old vessel, the *Discovery*, and the *Resolution*. His instructions, oddly enough, make no mention of searching for Henry Hudson and the other men who had been cast adrift the year before. Once he had sailed through Hudson Strait, he was to head directly west. And so he merely paused for a few days at Digges Island to set up a pinnace which he had brought out in frame, then shaped his course towards the Orient. He raised the west coast of Hudson Bay at about 60°40' north, however, between the present settlements of Churchill and Eskimo Point. Feeling his way carefully south, he finally wintered in the mouth of a river which he named the Nelson after Robert Nelson, master of the *Resolution*, who died and was buried there. Because Button's journal was never published, most of the details of his wintering have been lost; but we do know that it was a harsh winter, during which many of the men died from what was presumably a combination of scurvy and trichinosis.

In 1613 the ice broke up in the Nelson River on 21 April. It was another two months, however, before the bay was sufficiently clear of ice for the search for the elusive passage to be continued. When at last the ships could get out into the bay, they coasted north along the western shore, sailing deep into Roe's Welcome, on the west side of Southampton Island, before returning to England. Button was the first European to sight the western shores of Hudson Bay and thus to show that Hudson had discovered a vast inland sea—a new mediterranean—rather than the northeast corner of the Pacific Ocean. And even though he was unable to find a passage leading westward from Hudson's inland sea, Button was convinced that such a passage did exist.

The merchant adventurers who had financed the search for the northwest passage were also convinced and immediately set about fielding a new expedition to Hudson Bay. This time they selected Capt. William Gibbons to lead the party. Gibbons was a cousin of Thomas Button and had sailed with him on the previous voyage to the bay. The Gibbons expedition left England in March 1614, sailing in the same vessel—the *Discovery*—that had been used for arctic exploration by both Hudson and Button, and before them by George Weymouth in 1602. Even with that stout and courageous vessel to help him, Gibbons was unable to force his way through the unusually heavy ice which choked up the entrance to Hudson Strait that season. As he battled helplessly against a sea of ice, the Labrador Current slowly pushed him to the south. At about 58°30' north latitude he finally took refuge in a small bay on the coast of Labrador, where he was trapped by the ice for ten weeks. When he was finally released from the bay, which his crew referred to as "Gibbons' Hole", he sailed quietly back to England. It had not been a prosperous summer.

But the merchant adventurers were still not discouraged and calmly set about fielding yet another expedition to search for the northwest passage. This time they selected Robert Bylot as leader, with William Baffin as pilot. With a crew of fourteen men and two boys, they dropped down the Thames on 16 April 1615. By 6 May they were off the coast of Greenland, just east of Cape Farewell. They had trouble with the ice as they approached the entrance to Hudson Strait, not an uncommon experience in that locality where the Labrador Current brings vast quantities of ice sweeping down from Baffin Bay, far to the north. They worked their way through the ice, however, and finally entered the strait. Even there, there were vast quantities of drifting ice, but Bylot and his men were able to pick their way along the southern coast of what is now Baffin Island. At the western end of the strait they moved up into Foxe Basin, exploring the north and east coasts of Southampton Island. But the basin was packed with drifting ice, the weather was bad, and they saw little hope of a passage that way; and so they shaped their course for home, passing Resolution Island on 5 August and anchoring in Plymouth Sound on 7 September.

The London merchants were finally convinced that the northwest passage must lie far up the strait which John Davis had discovered and explored almost thirty years before. The following year, therefore, they sent Bylot and Baffin up through Davis Strait in that same indomitable vessel, the *Discovery*.

The Danes, meanwhile, had been developing their whaling industry in Spitzbergen, far to the north of Lapland, and exploring the coasts of Greenland. Like the English, the French, and the Dutch, the Danes were anxious to share in the vast riches that were being generated by trade with the Orient. King Christian IV of Denmark and Norway had taken an active part in the expansion of Danish industry and trade and must have watched England's repeated probes into arctic America with great interest. In any event, he decided to launch his own expedition and selected as its leader one of Denmark's most experienced seamen, Captain Jens Munk.

Jens Munk was born on 3 June 1579 on his father's estate near the modern town of Arendal in southern Norway. At that time, too, both

Denmark and Norway were under a single ruler—Frederik II, King of Denmark. The Munk family had at one time been members of the nobility, but Jens's grandfather, Niels Munk, had been stripped of his rank because of an improper alliance with a bondswoman. Had he simply lived with the woman, his behaviour might have been tolerated. It might have been overlooked even in a society which was reeling under the impact of the Reformation, with its associated puritanism. But when he actually married her, the king had no choice but to strip him of his patent of nobility. A nobleman at that time had to marry a woman who was also of noble birth if he wanted his title to pass on to his descendants.

Although Niels Munk lost his patent of nobility, he was permitted to retain Bordo, his estate near Arendal. In time it was passed on to his son Erik, who spent much of his life trying to win back the patent of nobility that his father had lost. Erik was an able leader of armies and fleets, as well as a competent administrator. But like his father before him, he tended to be unorthodox in his domestic arrangements; when he finally settled into the family estate at Bordo, it was not with a lawfully wedded wife but with Ann, the daughter of a barber from Elsinore. As a result, Jens was illegitimate. His father, meanwhile, was granted extensive fiefdoms for the many services that he had performed in defence of the realm and was finally knighted in 1581. By that time, however, Erik Munk had built up a rather unsavoury reputation as a harsh landlord. In addition, he was charged both with diverting crown property to his own personal use and with a variety of frauds. As a result, on 30 September 1585 he was stripped of all the lands he held in fief, and a royal vessel carried him to Copenhagen and to prison.

Ann and her illegitimate offspring were left stranded and penniless in a community that was openly hostile. With no way of keeping her small family together, Ann sent Jens to Aalborg, in Jutland, where he lived with his father's sister and her husband.

When he was only twelve years old, Jens returned to Norway, where he signed on with a Friesland skipper for a voyage to England and Portugal. He stayed there for a year, living with the family of an Oporto merchant named Duart Duez and learning Portuguese. In 1592, when he was still only thirteen years old, he worked his passage to Brazil as cabin-boy on a trading vessel. He remained in Brazil for six years, working at a number of different jobs. At one time he was apprenticed to a shoemaker; at another he was assistant to a portrait painter. Finally he joined the establishment of a merchant named Miguel Duez, the brother of Duart Duez with whom he had lived in Oporto. Leaving Brazil in 1598, he returned to Denmark, where he learned that his father had ended his long residence in a Danish prison by committing suicide.

Jens Munk never explained his wanting to learn Portuguese or his extended absence from his native land. In all probability, however, he was trying to escape the social and economic handicaps which he faced at home as the penniless and illegitimate son of a disgraced father. Whatever the reasons, they were apparently legitimate, for when he returned to Denmark he found immediate employment as a clerk, or book-keeper, on a merchant vessel. Over the next few years he criss-crossed western Europe, travelling back and forth to England, Spain, Holland, and the Baltic ports. By 1605 he was commanding a trading vessel of which he was part owner. A few years later he sailed to Iceland, where he picked up a cargo of sulphur from the rich deposits at Husavik. Then he went trading to Nova Zembla. In 1610 he again headed for Nova Zembla, this time in command of the *Angelibrand*, a vessel belonging to King Christian IV. He was ordered by his monarch to land a consignment of trade-goods at Kildin, a small outpost in Lapland, and then to explore the west coast of Nova Zembla as far north as 76° if ice conditions would permit him to attain such a high latitude. He was then to shape his course to the south and sail into the Kara Sea through Weygatz Straits, which separate Nova Zembla from the Siberian coast. The weather was particularly bad that year, however, and the northern seas were thickly choked with ice. Although Munk tried to force his way through the heavy pack, he had no choice but to return to Kildin, where he loaded his ship with a cargo of fish and headed for home.

When war broke out with Sweden the following spring, Munk joined the Danish navy on 1 March 1611, as a captain. He served as a naval officer for five years, then retired from the service to enter the whaling industry. Although the whale fishery of Spitzbergen was just beginning to emerge as a profitable venture, neither Denmark nor Norway had taken much notice of it. True, their proximity to the whaling grounds gave them a decided advantage over their rivals from England and Holland, but there was one serious problem. No one in Denmark, or in all of northern Europe for that matter, had any experience in whaling; and the taking of the large mammals required some highly skilled and experienced men, as did the flensing of such huge beasts and the extraction of the oil and whalebone. The only Europeans who possessed such skills were the Basques, who had been taking whales in the Bay of Biscay for centuries. In fact, they had virtually exterminated the Biscay whale when the rich whaling grounds around Spitzbergen were reported by William Barents and Henry Hudson. Munk therefore left Denmark in November 1616 for St. Jean de Luz, headquarters of the Basque whalers, to recruit the experienced men who could instruct the Danes in this new craft. He and his partners thus founded the Danish whaling industry. Munk maintained an interest in the Spitzbergen whale fishery for three years, and he apparently made one voyage there, in 1617.

Such, in brief, was the background of the man who was chosen by King Christian IV to search for a northwest passage. He was to follow in the wake of the English explorers—Hudson, Button, and Bylot—and with God's assistance was to overtake and outdistance them on the road to the Spice Islands. Munk was chosen, in all probability, because he was the most highly qualified man in the Danish navy. He was brave, experienced in arctic navigation, versatile, and trustworthy—fine qualities in any leader—and an excellent choice for the task that lay ahead.

Munk left Copenhagen on 9 May 1619 with two vessels, the *Unicorn* and the *Lamprey*, and a crew of sixty-four men. Sixteen months later, on 21 September 1620, he arrived back in Norway with only two men still alive. The rest had been buried in the small cove on the shores of Hudson Bay where he had wintered, opposite the present town of Churchill, Manitoba. The fearful mortality which had beset the crew was probably a combination of scurvy and trichinosis, made even more ghastly by exposure. The Danes had been totally unprepared for the rigours of a Canadian winter. After all, at 59° north Munk's wintering place was some seventy-five miles farther south than Bergen, Norway, and the entire Norwegian coast is ice-free, even as far north as North Cape and the ancient fortress of Vardo. What was not known at the time, of course, was that the coasts of northern Europe were washed by the soothing waters of the Gulf Stream. At Churchill, on the other hand, Munk and his party were exposed to the full, unmitigated fury of an arctic winter.

On the return voyage Munk had spent sixty-seven days aboard the *Lamprey*, and he must have looked forward to the comforts and tranquillity of his native land. But it was not to be. A few days after they landed, one of his sailors stabbed a man during a bar-room brawl. Munk, as captain of the vessel, was responsible for the conduct of his men, both afloat and ashore, and he was arrested. By the end of the month he was imprisoned in

Bergen. He was only released when the king ordered him to Copenhagen to report on the voyage to the northwest. As the king had already been told of the loss of his frigate and almost all of his men, however, Munk moved very slowly. As a result, he did not reach Copenhagen till Christmas Eve.

In spite of the fact that Munk was ill and exhausted, he was ordered to assemble men and equipment for another assault on the northwest passage. His surviving records show that his first concern was to correct the deficiencies of the first voyage. He would have the men dressed in sheepskin clothing to withstand the rigours of an arctic winter; he would feed them smoked meat rather than salt meat; and, above all, he would have surgeons who were acquainted with scurvy and who knew how to cure it. With the king's authority all this could be done. The story of Munk's first voyage had spread rapidly throughout Scandinavia, however, and volunteers for a second voyage to that remote and horrifying land simply could not be found. By the summer of 1621 the project had been abandoned.

Jens Munk spent the rest of his life in the service of King Christian IV. In November 1621 he was sent to Holland to recruit men for the Danish East India Company. The following year he was in Norway levying sailors for the fleet, and then, as captain of a man-of-war, he convoyed an East Indiaman as far as the Canary Islands. On his return he joined a naval squadron which escorted the king to Norway. In 1623 he took four warships to northern Norway and Lapland to stop the Russians from interfering with Danish traders in the area. His constant absences apparently led to domestic problems, for he divorced his wife, Kathrine Andersdatter, that same year. Munk's journal, *Navigatio Septentrionalis*, was published the following year, but again he was at sea in the service of the king he had served so long: he was in Pomerania hiring ships' carpenters; in Mecklenburg delivering a large sum of money to Duke Ulrich, the brother of King Christian; in the Baltic guarding against pirates and unlicensed foreign vessels.

In 1625, when Denmark was drawn into the Thirty Years' War, Munk was appointed admiral of a fleet of six vessels and was stationed off the mouth of the Weser, blockading the port of Bremen. One of his ships was his old sloop, the *Lamprey*, which was lost with all hands. Munk spent the next three summers off the mouth of the Weser, returning each fall to Copenhagen, where he spent the winter. Then, in early April 1628, he was wounded either at Fehmern or at Kiel, and he returned to Copenhagen aboard the *Lobster*. He landed on 16 April and died about two months later. The exact date is not known.

In preparing this manuscript for publication, my only aim has been to make a little-known paragraph in the history of Canada available to the general public. Scholars, after all, have access to Munk's story in Volume XCVII of the Hakluyt Society publications and to other technical references and summaries scattered throughout the literature on arctic exploration. But this material, by and large, is not available to the more casual reader, nor is it available to that turbulent stream of students who want—or are told—to learn more of our early history. If this is accepted, then, by the general reader, my efforts will not have been wasted; for I have not tried to add anything to the sum of human knowledge but have laboured only to make a small portion of that knowledge more readily available. I have therefore been very frugal with my editorial comments and have intruded as gently as possible into Munk's narrative. This new version of the narrative itself — by permission of the Hakluyt Society, which I gratefully acknowledge — is based on C.C.A. Gosch's translation, published in 1897.

While working on the "Jens Munk Project", I was kindly assisted by the staff of the Department of Indian and Northern Affairs in Churchill, Manitoba, particularly Miss M.J. Cox, Area Superintendent, and Mr. Bernard Potvin, Interpretation Officer. In Winnipeg I met with Mrs. Shirlee A. Smith, Hudson's Bay Company Archivist, Mrs. Helen Burgess, Editor of *The Beaver*, and Robert V. Oleson, Secretary of the Hudson's Bay Record Society. As always, I found our discussions both pleasant and profitable. And in my own office I enjoyed the continued assistance of Miss Peta Daniels, Miss Kathy Mills, and Mrs. Carol Barton. For such generous support I am extremely grateful.

THE JOURNAL OF JENS MUNK 1619–1620

In the Year of
Our Lord 1619

Following the orders of His Most Gracious Majesty King Christian IV of Denmark, the royal ships *Unicorn* and *Lamprey* were made ready for a voyage through the northwest passage. They were provided with crews, equipment, provisions, ammunition, and everything else that would be required for such a venture. I, Jens Munk, sailed the two ships from Copenhagen into the Sound on 9 May with a crew of sixty-four men—forty-eight in the *Unicorn* and sixteen in the *Lamprey*. Before I could leave the Sound, however, I had to wait for a wind till Whitsunday, 16 May.

Two days later, as we were cruising along in the early morning, a sailor who was walking around on deck suddenly jumped overboard. He leaped out about two fathom and dived headfirst into the water, but did not appear to sink as quickly as he hoped. Because it was blowing hard at the time, we were unable to save him, so he went down and was lost.

On 25 May, when we were off the island of Lister, the sloop sprang a leak, forcing us to run into Karmsund for repairs. When I examined the hull, I found that three bolt holes had been left open by the carpenters and had later been plugged with pitch. I had this defect corrected as quickly as possible so that I could continue the voyage. While we were staying at Karmsund, one of my two coopers died, so I hired three lads from Skudenes in order to maintain my full complement of men.[1] Then, on 30 May, we shaped our course west-northwest for the Shetland Islands, which we passed on 2 June.

On the morning of 4 June we sailed past Sydneröe, the southernmost of the Faerö Islands, continued for about 16 or 18 miles, then headed west and west by north.

---

[1] Only two men were actually reported lost, the cooper and the sailor who jumped overboard.

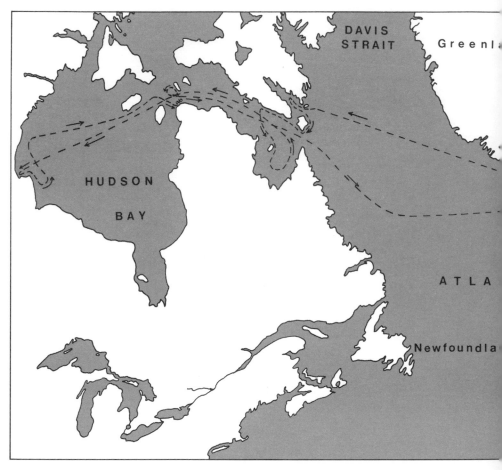

Jens Munk's route 1619-1620

On 11 June I calculated how much of our provisions had already been used up and issued instructions as to how the remaining provisions were to be rationed. The steward's book, listing the provisions that he received, was to be kept in the cabin, and whenever he opened a barrel of supplies, he was to enter it in the book. He was to make a weekly report in which he stated how long each barrel lasted, giving both the day and the hour when it was finished. He was also to report either the weight or the volume of all

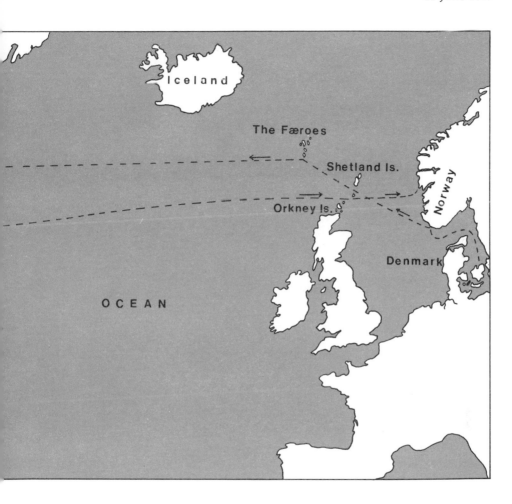

provisions consumed, depending upon whether they were solids or liquids. And all provisions were to be issued by the steward in accordance with regulations that I laid down for the feeding of the men, and which I would change from time to time, as circumstances might require. In this way I would always have an accurate account of what had been consumed and what we still had on hand.

We continued thus on a westerly course till 20 June, when we raised the east coast of Greenland at 61°25′ north. When we were still about 15 or

16 miles from land, we encountered so much ice that we were forced to turn eastwards again. We were then caught up in gales and foul weather till the thirtieth, when we sighted the southern tip of Greenland, which the English call Cape Farewell, at 60°30' north.[1] This southern promontory of Greenland is rugged and uneven, with high, jagged mountains. It was impossible to make an accurate sketch of the coast because it was covered by such a vast quantity of ice.

Once we were past Cape Farewell, we entered Davis Strait, which was also jammed with ice. The reason for all the ice in that area is this: the east coast of Greenland trends generally to the northeast so that all of the ice that comes streaming along the coast is moving in a southwesterly direction. The west coast of Greenland, on the other hand, trends generally to the northwest, as does Davis Strait itself. From that coast of Greenland, too, comes an unspeakable quantity of ice flowing in a southeasterly direction. This abundance of floating ice emerges from the numerous large fjords on both coasts of Greenland. Both streams of ice, then, meet off Cape Farewell, which projects southward like the point of a triangle.

In Davis Strait much ice is also encountered on the American side, where a vessel may easily be driven off course by a current that sets generally to the southwest. Anyone who intends to sail into the strait, therefore, must do so at 62°30' north and, if possible, take his departure from Cape Farewell itself. He must be particularly careful, too, in working out his variation, otherwise he will steer a wrong course. Thus the navigator must know both his latitude and the precise variation.

But let me return to my own voyage. As soon as I was free of the ice at the Cape, I set a course west by north, true, allowing two points for variation. We encountered a great deal of ice, some of it in large masses rising almost 40 fathom out of the sea, but were able to work our way through it because we were in open water. To those who have never seen such things, this account may sound incredible, but it is true, nevertheless.

On 8 July we sighted land on the American side of the strait but were unable to go ashore because of the great quantity of ice along the coast. At noon our latitude was 62°30' north,[2] and we were standing off and on

---

[1] Cape Farewell is at 59°45'N, 43°53' W.

[2] At that latitude, he would be opposite Christopher Hall Island. That is, he was in Davis Strait, just north of the entrance to Frobisher Bay.

The Grinnell Glacier and Wynne Edwards Bay, one of the three "Ice Fjords" off Frobisher Bay referred to by Munk in his journal. ROM photograph.

outside the ice without being able to accomplish anything. During the night of 9 July there was a dense fog, and it was so cold that there were six-inch icicles hanging from the rigging. Before three o'clock the next afternoon, however, the sun had grown so hot that the men threw off their overcoats, and some of them discarded their jackets as well. Finally I stood in amongst the ice till I found myself in a great bay.[1] The pilots said that according to our latitude we were probably in the entrance to Hudson Strait, but after a detailed examination we discovered that this was not so. We were in a bay where great quantities of ice come out of three large fjords, and thus we named the place Iisefiorde (i.e., Ice Fjords). Its latitude is 62°30' north, and it extends as far as Resolution Island, trending south-southeast, half south, and north-northwest, half north. We shaped our course southerly along this coast, which we found to consist entirely of broken ground and huge rocks, till we came to Resolution. This island marks the north side of the entrance to Hudson Strait.

---

[1] He was now in Frobisher Bay.

7

Although there was a great deal of ice floating around, 11 July was a beautiful sunny day, so that it was possible for us to obtain the precise latitude of Resolution—61°21' north. In my instructions the island which marks the south side of the entrance to Hudson Strait, Button Island, was said to be situated at 62°30' north; we found, however, that its latitude is only 60°40' north. There may possibly be an error in this figure, however, as we could not get very close to the island because of the ice. Before I describe the things that happened to us as we moved through Hudson Strait, let me issue a general warning to anyone who might follow us through that passage: do not drop below 61°30' north as you approach the strait or you will be pushed off course by a powerful current that sets toward the south. And note, too, that there is a strong ebb flowing from the strait itself, where the water, which is very deep, rises and falls at least five fathom during an ordinary tide.

On 12 July I sent my lieutenant, Mauritz Stygge, ashore at Resolution with some of the crew to fetch water and to see if he could find an anchorage. When he returned with the water that evening, he reported that there were harbours in the area, but that there was no anchorage nor was there any place where we could lie in safety from the ice. We were therefore obliged to choose between dangerous alternatives because we could find neither open water nor a safe anchorage. Half a mile from Resolution we heaved the lead and found bottom at 150 fathom. That same day I shot two or three birds, and on the last shot the gun burst, slicing the brim off the front of my hat.

By late afternoon on the thirteenth our position became perilous when the ice pressed us hard on all sides, making it impossible for us to either advance or retreat. The officers agreed that the best thing to do under the circumstances was to fasten the two vessels together and let them drift with the ice. And so, trusting to God's merciful assistance, that was done.

While we were drifting around in this manner, a great block of ice displaced the main knee of the *Unicorn*. This knee, which supports the beak-head of the vessel, was fastened with six large iron bolts. I immediately set all my carpenters to straightening it, but because it was so large and heavy, and because it was set outside the hull, they were unable to do anything with it. I therefore had the ship turned so that the side of the bow to which the knee had been displaced drifted against the ice. I then worked the rudder so that the ice could shove the knee back into its original position. This was done as perfectly as if twenty carpenters had been engaged in refitting it; all that remained to be done was to adjust the bolts that were bent.

By daybreak on 15 July we were finally out of the ice and continuing our westward voyage. We followed the northern shore of the strait, tacking from time to time under the high coastline to leeward. Later in the day, when the wind shifted around to the east, we shaped our course to the northwest, sailing between the main body of ice and the shore and spreading only our small sails. There seemed to be good harbours in several places along the coast, but they were all filled with ice, and as there was ice drifting about us on all sides, I did not dare to send my boat ashore to look for a safe anchorage. Late in the day, however, we came to some small islands which stretched away from the mainland in a more westerly direction. Here we again encountered much ice, which kept us outside the islands till 17 July. Finally I ordered the sloop to sail ahead of us to see if she could lead the *Unicorn* to a safe anchorage. In this way and with God's assistance, we found a snug harbour where we could drop our anchor.

The following day I sent some of the men to search the surrounding area to see if they could find any of the natives. They returned around noon without having met anyone but reported that there were signs of people having been there, although none of the signs was fresh. In the afternoon, while the vessels were hidden behind a small island, we noticed some people on the south side of the harbour, so I had my boat manned as quickly as possible and went to meet them. When they saw that I intended to land, they hid their weapons and other implements behind some rocks and just stood waiting. When I did land, they returned my salutation, but they were careful to stay between me and the place where they had hidden their arms. However, I had made careful note of where their weapons were, so I went over, picked them up, and examined them. While I was looking them over, the natives led me to believe that they would rather lose all their clothing and be forced to go naked than lose their weapons. Pointing to their mouths, they indicated that they used the weapons to procure their food. When I finally laid down their weapons, they clapped their hands, looked up to heaven, and seemed overjoyed. I then presented them with knives and all sorts of other iron goods. In addition, I gave one of them a looking-glass, but he didn't know what it was. When I took it from him and held it in front of his face so that he could see himself, he grabbed the glass and hid it under his clothing. After that, the natives gave me presents of everything they had, including different kinds of birds, and

This picture represents two separate episodes from Munk's journal. In the distance Munk and his men encounter native people. In the foreground they are seen hunting reindeer. From *Danish Arctic Expeditions, 1605-1620*, ed. C.C.A. Gosch. Courtesy of the Hakluyt Society.

seal meat. All the natives embraced one of my men who had a swarthy complexion and black hair—they thought, no doubt, that he was one of their countrymen.

We set sail that same evening and by the following day were again standing off and on at the ice-front. As I had no hope of getting through the ice at that time, I returned to the harbour we had just left, because I was anxious to see more of the natives. But it was not to be. Although I remained there till 22 July, none of the natives appeared, in spite of the gifts we had given them, nor did they return to fetch their fishing gear, which was lying around all the time we were there. All this suggests that they were subject to some authority which had forbidden them to visit us again. While I remained in the harbour hoping that the ice would drift away, I ordered the crew to fetch water and wash their clothes. I also sent some of the men inland to shoot reindeer, which are plentiful in that area.

By late afternoon on 22 July I had decided that the natives were not going to reappear, and so I prepared to sail. First, however, I erected the arms of His Royal Majesty King Christian IV and named the harbour that had sheltered us "Reindeer Sound" because we had shot so many reindeer there. At every spot where the natives had left their fish-nets, we deposited various items such as knives and other iron tools just before we set sail. That harbour, incidentally, is a very good one because it is protected on all sides.

The following morning at daybreak we found ourselves completely surrounded by ice. We made the *Lamprey* fast to the *Unicorn* at both bow and stern and brought down the topmasts when the winds were approaching gale force. Then we drifted wherever the wind and the ice might carry us, with no open water visible anywhere. During the following night we were so firmly jammed in the ice that four anchors were crushed on the bow of the *Lamprey*. At the same time, the pressure of the ice had raised the sloop so far out of the water that you could pass your hand along the entire length of the keel from stem to stern.

On 24 July we were still trapped in the ice. Between our vessels and the shore the ice was solid, while in the offing the sea-ice was pressed firmly against us by a southeast gale. On the twenty-fifth we were still caught in the ice, without any open water in sight. That same day I almost lost two men who were trying to bring back a grapnel from a large mass of ice. We had hooked the *Unicorn* to the mass of ice in order to swing her around so that she would not be carried away by the strong current that was running. During the process we also smashed the housing of the *Unicorn*'s rudder-head. That night the ice and the current carried us in between the mainland and some small islands so smoothly that even ten pilots who had navigated vessels through that channel year after year could not have done it more expertly.

All the next day we were hemmed in so tightly by the ice that we could neither set an anchor in the ground nor run a hawser ashore. The ship, however, remained in the same place all day, drifting neither one way nor the other, and we were in great danger. As there was nothing we could do to alleviate our distress, we commended the whole matter into the hands of God and prayed devoutly to Him for help and guidance. We also gave something for the poor, each according to his means.

On 27 July we were still among the islands, drifting on shore with one tide and off again with the next, and there was so much ice around us that it would have been impossible to get a boat ashore, even if our lives had depended on it. On 28 July, after much trouble, we finally succeeded in entering a little bay between two small islands. We immediately let go three anchors and carried two hawsers ashore. When the tide went out, we were so close to shore that there was scarcely any water left under our keel; but when the tide came in, we were so battered by the ice that we had to work much harder there in our harbour than we ever did when we were caught in the ice at sea. While we were anchored, a large mass of ice, which was grounded in 22 fathom of water, suddenly split in two. Its collapse raised such huge waves that the *Lamprey* was almost put ashore. The sloop was fastened to the side of the *Unicorn* at the time, but we quickly got her clear of the ship. We lost one anchor, which was smashed against the bow of the *Unicorn* before we could cut the anchor rope, but suffered no other damage.

During the next two days we spent all our time trying to keep the ice from damaging the vessels. Then, on the thirty-first, a particularly high tide carried us over some rocks towards shore. At low tide the rocks were left high and dry, rising some four fathom above water and leaving us in a small bay where we were well protected from the ice. This was fortunate, because the men were completely exhausted; they could not have continued the incredible labour of pushing vast quantities of ice from the vessels or the incessant veering and hauling.

By the following day, 1 August, when the crew was somewhat rested and the vessels were riding safely at anchor, I took a quarter of the men ashore to hunt reindeer. Although we saw a few, they were so very shy that we could not get near them. Meanwhile the men who had remained with the ships had not been idle but had worked steadily at fending off the ice so as to protect the vessels.

It was not till 5 August that the ice began to disperse and I could see some hope of leaving. In preparation, I trimmed the hold and took on more ballast and fresh water. I also put the beer into fresh casks. When everything was ready, I issued new orders regarding the places and latitudes where we would meet if we should become separated in the fog, although such a meeting would be a very uncertain matter.

On 8 August so much snow fell that the mountains were completely covered and more than six inches piled up on the deck. On that same day I buried a seaman named Anders Staffuanger. We called our harbour "Rabbit Sound" because we caught so many rabbits there. We also set up His Royal Majesty's arms and name on large cairns. This harbour is situated almost 50 miles inside Hudson Strait, on the north side; its latitude is 62°20' north. It is situated close to a large bay which stretches off to the north. A short distance to the west is another bay which also stretches off to the north. Because of the great quantity of ice that was drifting about while we were anchored at Rabbit Sound, it was not possible to travel even an eighth of a mile from the ship by boat, so the bays were never explored. On the shores of the sound there is much Muscovy Glass[1] and there seemed to be some ore; but as I had no one with me who had any knowledge of such matters, we could do very little about it. All I could do was fill some barrels with the supposed ore and take them on board. We saw none of the country people while we were there, although we saw a great many places where they had pitched their tents in the past.

Continuing our journey on 9 August, we set sail with a northwest wind, shaping our course west-southwest, which was as near to the wind as we could sail.[2] Fortunately, we were clear of the ice by then, except for a few pieces which were still drifting about. By the time we got out into the strait, a stiff gale was blowing, which raised a high and hollow sea such as no one on board had ever witnessed before. It was caused by the tide and the wind acting against each other when there was a gale of wind blowing, for in that area the water rises and falls over five fathom with an ordinary tide.

In the early morning of 10 August we reached what the men thought was the western end of Hudson Strait, where the pilot shaped our course to the south. He thought we had arrived at Hudson Bay, but we soon found that this was not so. As we sailed along the shore in a southerly direction, we found the land to be very high, broken, and girt with many islands. No doubt we would have found fine harbours there if we had taken the time to search for them. We came at last to the large promontory that lies in about 60° north, and which we called "Auk's Cape". There we entered a large bay stretching due southwest and leading to a low, flat land which the English pilot thought was the place we were searching for. He soon had to swallow both his words and his opinion, however. Some fine

---

[1] Mica.

[2] That is, he could sail no closer than 67°30', or six points, to the wind.

inlets appeared to open into the bay, but we had no time to explore them as we had to continue our voyage. We named the place "Southern Bay"; it is situated in 60° north, or a little more southerly.

On 14 August, when we had sailed nearly five miles out of the bay, we came to a large island. Its northwestern extremity was very high, its southern shore was packed with ice, and there were a great many birds in the area. Because it was covered with snow, we named it "Snow Island".

When the wind shifted to the east on 20 August, we shaped our course west by north, true, when we were at 62°20' north. We were then back in the strait, but it was so foggy we could not see land on either side, although the channel was not more than 16 miles wide at that spot. Thus we continued sailing until we were at 63°20' north. Meanwhile we had visited several places which are not named here, but which are diligently described and illustrated on the sea-chart which has been prepared to show their dimensions, quantity, quality, size, and shape.[1]

At the west end of Hudson Strait a pilot must be extremely cautious, because the currents from both the strait and Hudson Bay meet there. As a result, there is a great deal of turbulence in the area, as well as a great deal of drifting ice which cannot escape in either direction; it simply drifts away with one tide and comes back with the next. About ten miles inside the turbulent area there are two islands called "Digges Islands", named after Sir Dudley Digges by Henry Hudson, who discovered them in 1610. A pilot may feel his way around them by sounding. If he wishes to sail directly to Jens Munk's Bay, however, he should leave the islands half a mile or a mile to port, although it is perfectly safe to run on either side of them. Proceeding westward, he will then come to a large, flat, low island called Mansel Island,[2] around which he may also sail by sounding, as I did. It is a great pity that this island is not situated in a southern latitude because it is a large, flat land. Although a pilot may run on either side of it when entering Hudson Bay, it is better to keep to the north as there is less ice there than on the south side.

From the northern point of Mansel Island to Jens Munk's Bay the course is southwest by south and southwest, and the distance is three days' and three nights' sailing. As soon as the sounding lead finds bottom

---

[1] This chart has not survived.

[2] Mansel Island was named by Thomas Button in 1613 after Sir Robert Mansel, treasurer of the navy.

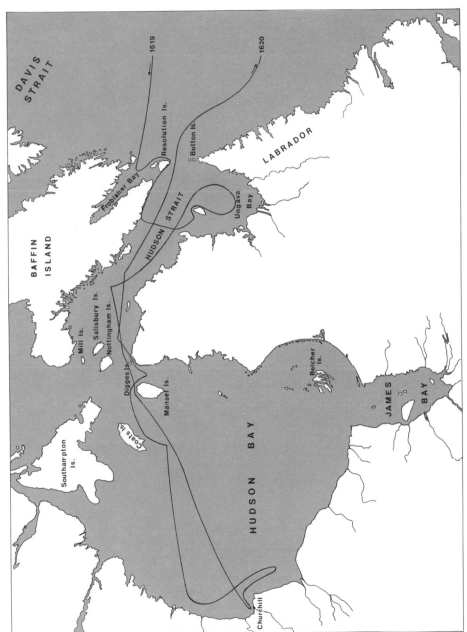

Hudson Bay

at 30 fathom, the pilot should shape his course a bit more to the south till he sights the southern shore, which is low and wooded. Next will appear some low rocks which form a narrow promontory, on which I erected two beacons. To enter the harbour, steer southwest, keeping the beacons to starboard. A short distance inside the harbour is a sunken rock, but it is on the eastern side and can be passed without any difficulty. The pilot may then cast his anchor in seven or eight fathom. My wintering place can be found easily, because the *Unicorn* (for reasons which will be explained later) is lying there about a mile farther up the river, behind a promontory on the western side.

When I first entered the harbour at my wintering place on 7 September 1619, it was with great difficulty, because there were high winds, with snow, hail, and fog. Once inside, I had the men assemble the shallop which we had in frame, that is, divided into six pieces so that it could be carried more easily aboard the ship. During the following night we kept watch on land and kept a fire going as a signal to the *Lamprey*, which had become separated from us in a great storm. She joined us on the ninth, having been under the northern land, where a passage was supposed to exist, but where none could be found. Because of the bad weather as well as other hardships, some of the crew were ill, so I had them taken ashore. There we gathered cloudberries and gooseberries and the ones that are called *tydebaer*[1] and *kragbear*[2] in Norway. I also built a good fire on shore for the comfort of the sick. Then, such a terrible snowstorm raged through the tenth and eleventh that there was very little we could do.

Early the next morning a large white bear came down to the water's edge, where it started to eat a beluga fish that I had caught the day before. I shot the bear and gave the meat to the crew with orders that it was to be just slightly boiled, then kept in vinegar overnight. I even had two or three pieces of the flesh roasted for the cabin. It was of good taste and quite agreeable.

On 13 September I sent out both the shallop and the ship's boat to see what accommodation the land afforded and whether there were any better harbours than the one we were in. The boats were commanded by my second mates, Hans Brock and Jan Pettersen, who had been told to follow the coast for eight or nine miles, one to the west of our anchorage and the

---

[1] Cowberry or mountain cranberry (*Vaccinium vitisidaea*)
[2] Crowberry (*Empetrum nigrum L*)

The west bank of the Churchill River near its mouth, about four miles downstream from Munk's wintering place. Photo courtesy of the Hudson's Bay Company.

other to the east. Pettersen returned on 16 September to report that no harbours had been found to the west. The coast there was low, flat, and wooded, he said, with few places where even a ship's boat could be properly protected. On the day he returned, there was a terrible snowstorm from the northeast.

As it was still cold and snowing on the eighteenth, I gathered my officers together to discuss our situation and to decide what we should do about it. We finally agreed that our best plan in those unfavourable circumstances would be to move the ship in behind some promontory where she would be safe from drifting ice; for winter was almost upon us.

On 19 September we sailed both the ship and the sloop up the river as far as we could, then dropped anchor. During the night the newly formed ice cut into the hulls of the vessels, leaving gashes that were almost two fingers deep. I was obliged, as a result, to work the ship across a tidal flat till she was about eight cable-lengths closer to the western shore. The flat itself was some 900 fathom wide. While we were moving the ship across the flat, she was in great danger because the area was covered with rocks. In addition, she would not rest comfortably on the bottom at low tide, because she was sharp built instead of having the low, broad bilges that would have kept her upright. At one point she was caught by the ice and driven on a rock, where she sprang such a leak that the carpenter barely had time to repair it before the next high tide.

By 25 September we had secured the ship in close under the land and floated the sloop ashore on a high tide. I then had the ship's keel dug down into the ground and piled branches close under both sides of the vessel. These I packed in with clay and sand so that the vessel would be evenly supported and thus would suffer less damage. Hans Brock, who returned that same day, reported that there were no harbours suitable for winter quarters in any of the places he had seen, but only flat, bare, and swampy land. During his exploration he had nearly lost his life because of the quantity of sharp new ice which was floating around; and he did lose a grapnel on a foul bottom when the rope snapped.

By 27 September we believed that the ship was well protected against both drifting ice and foul weather. But then such a tremendous drift of ice came down upon us with an ebbing tide that if the ship had not been resting so firmly on the ground she would have been carried away. Although the ship was moored with four hawsers, the pressure of the ice was so great that they started to snap under the strain. As soon as the first one snapped, the others were quickly cast off. By the time the flood returned, the vessel had sprung a number of leaks and had taken on so much water that it took almost two thousand strokes to pump her dry. She had also been shifted out of the dock we had built around her.

At high tide the next day we warped the ship back into her dock, where we moored her with six hawsers, and at the lowest ebb of the next tide the leaks were found and stopped. Next, I put some of the men to repairing the dock, while the carpenters and anyone else who could ply an axe were put to building five piers, which I placed before the bow of the ship to deflect the ice that came drifting down the river. The rest of the men hauled timber and rocks. Everything was completed by 1 October, with both of the vessels protected against ice and storms. I also cleared out the

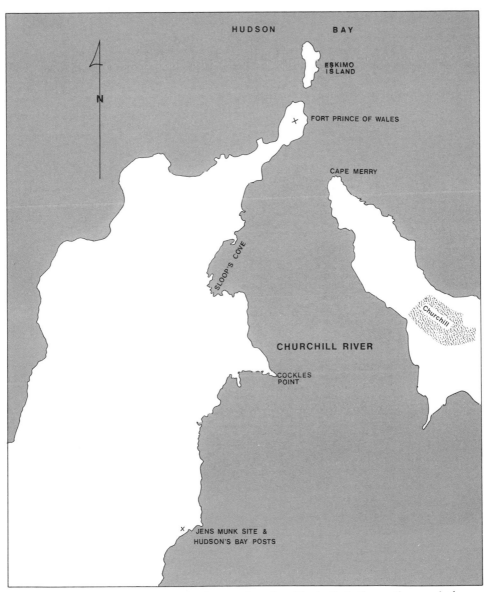

The mouth of the Churchill River. The distance from Jens Munk site to the southern end of Eskimo Island is about 4½ miles (7.3 km).

hold of the *Unicorn*, moved some of our gear ashore, and then placed all of the cannon in the empty hold. I did this to give us more room to move about and also to relieve the deck of the great weight of the cannon.

On 3 October I ordered the crew of the *Lamprey* to take their meals on the *Unicorn* so we would not have to keep two galleys going at the same time, and I gave strict orders to both the steward and the cook regarding the messing of the crews. These orders were based on the instructions I had received in Denmark but were modified to meet the requirements of that particular time and place. The next day I distributed clothes, shirts, shoes, and boots to the men, as well as anything else that I thought would help to protect them from the cold.

On 5 October I had two large fireplaces built on deck, each one so large that twenty men could sit around it comfortably. In the steerage I built another fireplace that would also accommodate twenty men. There was a fire in the galley as well, but the men could not warm themselves there because the cook needed all the space for his work. On 7 October, and for the next few days, the carpenters were ashore with the men, cutting timbers and hauling stones to build breakwaters. These were built to protect the ship from the ice which would occasionally bear down upon us in great masses while the tide was coming in and would continue to threaten us till the tide was half way out again.

As the seventh was a very fine day, I travelled up the river to see how far I could get in a small boat. About a mile and a half upstream there were so many rocks in the river-bed that we had to turn back. I had brought all manner of small items with me in the hope that we would meet some natives, and that by giving them gifts we would become better acquainted with them, but we didn't see a soul. On the way back to the ship I landed on a promontory where I found half of a devil drawn on a stone with charcoal. I named the place "Devil's Cape".

Although we did not see any natives, we saw traces of their summer camps in a number of different spots, including the place where our ship was docked. There were also many places in the forest where great heaps of woodchips were found. From the nature of the chips it looked as though the natives were cutting their wood with curved iron tools. I am of the opinion, too, that the natives practise some form of idolatry, for wherever we found their summer camps, we also found rectangles about eight feet square bordered with stones. One end of the square was always covered with flat stones and moss, while at the other end two thin, flat rocks would

Munk's men fell trees and build shelters. From *Danish Arctic Expeditions, 1605-1620*, ed. C.C.A. Gosch. Courtesy of the Hakluyt Society.

be set on edge about a foot apart, supporting a third flat stone. These appeared to be altars, particularly as two or three small pieces of charcoal were often found on the top of the structure, though there was no other evidence of fire in the area. From all these indications, I could only conclude that these places had been used for idolatrous worship, and if that is so, then it is to be wished that those poor blinded pagans might be led to accept the true Christian faith. Regarding their mode of living, it would seem that they eat much of their food in a half-cooked state, because the bones we found around their camps did not seem to have been roasted very well.

I started to ration the wine on 10 October, although I still let the men drink as much beer as they wished. I also issued regulations for the posting of sentinels, the fetching of wood, the burning of charcoal, and the melting

21

of snow for water. Thus each man knew what he was supposed to do and how he was to conduct himself.

During the night of 15 October the ice again shifted the *Unicorn* from her dock, forcing us to pack branches, clay, and sand under her bilges a second time. That same tide carried away one of the piers that we had built to protect the ship, so we immediately set about building a new one. A terribly hard frost finally froze us in solidly on the night of 22 October, after which the ship suffered no further damage. We caught a black fox that same night.

From that day on, the crew went ashore each day to hunt. Some of the men went into the forest, where they set traps for small animals and built small shelters to use as blinds. Others went to the more open country for shooting, as there were plenty of hares, ptarmigan, and other birds to be taken, so long as the snow was not too deep. Everyone enjoyed going ashore when the weather was good, for every time they went hunting they returned with game. Before Christmas, hunting was our main pastime.

Up to 3 October there was always some open water in the river because of the strong current that prevailed, but on that day the whole river finally froze over. Around that time, however, the frost was not too severe, and each day was clear and sunny. I took the opportunity, therefore, to go ashore with nineteen men on 7 November to see if we could find any of the natives. After we had penetrated only three miles into the country, a sudden great blanket of snow descended, making it too difficult for us to continue, so that we had to return without accomplishing anything. What we needed were skis such as are used in Norway and men who knew how to use them. With skis, we might have travelled far enough to meet some of the natives; without them, it was impossible to move around at all in that country during the winter.

On 10 November, which was St. Martin's Eve, the men shot some ptarmigan, with which we had to content ourselves instead of the traditional "St. Martin's Goose". To celebrate the occasion I issued a pint of Spanish wine to each mess in addition to the usual allowance, and the men cheered up considerably. And as usual, they could have as much of the ship's beer as they wanted. Later on, when the frost became sharper, the beer froze solid, so that I was afraid to let the men drink it without boiling it first. I therefore boiled every fresh barrel of beer as it was brought out to be used. This was better than snow-water for drinking or mixing with the wine. However, I let the men follow their own inclinations in this matter, for if they can get away with it, the common people are apt to do the very thing that is most strongly forbidden without worrying about whether it is good for them or not.

On 14 November two of the men went out to the blind that they had built in the forest, and during the first night they caught two black foxes and one cross fox, all of which had very beautiful fur.

On the night of the fifteenth the man who was on guard shot what he thought was a black fox and gleefully dragged it into the cabin, thinking he had a great prize. When we examined it in the morning, however, we found it was nothing but a large dog. The animal had apparently been trained to catch game, because the hair was rubbed off his muzzle where it had been tied with small cords. His right ear was cleft, and his owner would no doubt be very displeased to lose him. I should have been very pleased to catch him alive, for I would then have made a peddler of him and sent him home with a packet of small gifts.

Around 21 November the weather was very beautiful—as fine as could be expected in Denmark at that time of year—with open water as far as we could see in the bay outside our harbour. We noticed at that time that there is apparently no current in the bay, for the ice drifts around according to the strength of the wind. As long as the fine weather lasted, the men spent every day in the forest, even though the snow was very deep. Some of them shot ptarmigan, which are very good eating, while others looked after the traps, in which they caught a variety of small fur-bearing animals.

On 21 November we buried a sailor who had been ill for a long time. Two days later, when the sun was in the southwest, we noticed that there appeared to be three suns in the sky. Then, on the twenty-seventh, there was such a sharp frost that all the glass bottles that held our syrups and nostrums were shattered. It should be noted, therefore, that anyone who intends to travel in such cold regions should supply himself with bottles made of tin or some other substance that will resist the frost.

As the weather was very mild on 3 December, I went out in the estuary with some of the men to see how thick the ice was in the middle of the channel. We found that it was about three and a half feet thick. We later discovered that the ice remained that same thickness till long after Christmas, regardless of the temperature. In quiet standing water, however, it became much thicker. We noticed during our voyage, incidentally, that much of the ice that drifts forward and backward in the sea is extremely thick. Coming out of the large rivers and bays, this ice is joined together and piled up by the winds and currents and thus becomes quite thick. Amongst this ice, however, there are some huge masses rising as much as 20 fathom above the water.[1] When I examined some of these larger masses, I found that they were aground in water that was more than 40 fathom deep. This may seem incredible, but it is true nonetheless. It is my opinion that these very large masses of ice are formed in places where there are high mountains dropping steeply into very deep water. As the snow piles up on the mountains, it becomes heavier and heavier till it slides gradually down the mountains, enters the water, and is congealed into ice.

On 10 December, at about half past eight in the evening, there was an eclipse of the moon. Shortly after the moon rose that night, it was surrounded by a large, clear circle of light and divided into four equal parts by two lines, one vertical and one horizontal. This phenomenon first appeared when the moon was in the east-northeast and continued till it moved around to the east, where the eclipse started. At the beginning of the eclipse the moon was 15½° above the eastern horizon. When the eclipse ended, at ten o'clock, the moon bore southeast by south and was 47° above the southern horizon. For further information concerning this eclipse I refer the reader to the ephemerides, where he will find the exact time when the eclipse began and ended at home. He will then know precisely what difference there is between the longitudes of the two places. Such, then, is the short and simple description of the eclipse which I observed at my wintering place. I hope that the benevolent reader who understands these matters will look upon my efforts with charity, even though I have not been able to describe every aspect of the matter as I should have.

One of my two surgeons, David Velske of the *Lamprey*, died on 12 December. We had to keep his body on the ship for two days because the frost was so severe that no one could get ashore to bury him till the fourteenth, and even then the cold was of such intensity that many of the men had their faces frostbitten.

On 20 December the weather was so nice and mild that the whole crew went ashore. Some went hunting in order to get fresh meat for the Christmas Holy Days; the rest were cutting wood and burning charcoal.

---

[1] Here, Munk is making a general and fairly accurate observation on the formation of the icebergs which he had encountered earlier.

Those who were hunting returned in the evening with one hare and a number of ptarmigan. During a sharp frost on 22 December, I had a barrel filled with water, and when we knocked off the hoops in the morning, we found it was frozen solid. On Christmas Eve I gave the men some wine and strong beer, which they had to boil as it too was frozen. Although the men drank as much as they could hold, which made them quite hilarious, no one was at all offensive.

We celebrated the Holy Christmas Day solemnly, as is a Christian's duty, with a goodly sermon and a mass. After the sermon we gave the priest an offertory, as is the ancient custom, each according to his means. There was not much money among the men, but they gave what they had. So many of them gave white fox skins that the priest had enough of them to line his coat. A life long enough to wear it was not granted him, however. As the weather was mild during the Holy Days, the men played games to amuse themselves, and whoever could think up the most amusing game was the most popular. At the time the crew was in good health and brimming with merriment.

In the Year of
Our Lord 1620

On New Year's Day there was such a tremendously sharp frost that I issued a couple of pints of wine to each of the messes over and above their daily allowance, to keep the men's spirits up. It was a clear, sunny day with a northwest wind, a combination that always brought us the coldest weather. During the following days we had the worst weather we had experienced all winter and suffered more severely from that terrible frost than from anything else. That fearfully hard frost continued into the second week of January, with clear skies and a northwest wind. And on 8 January one of my sailors died. Then on the next day the men started catching some foxes and sables again.

On the tenth, Mr. Rasmus Jensen, the priest, and Mr. Casper Caspersen, the surgeon, took to their beds after having been ill for some time. That same day my head cook perished. And then a violent illness spread among the men, growing worse each day. It was a peculiar malady, in which the sick men were usually attacked by dysentery about three weeks before they died.

Around 18 January the weather was as mild as it is in Denmark at that time of year. All the men who were still healthy were working in the forest, mainly hunting ptarmigan to get fresh meat for the men who were sick. The weather was still clear and sunny on the twenty-first, but by that time thirteen of us were down with the sickness. Among them was the surgeon, Casper Caspersen, who was mortally ill by then. I approached him nonetheless, asking him, as I had asked so many times before, if there was not some medicine in his chest that would cure the men, or at least comfort them. He replied that he had already used every medicine he had with him and that without God's assistance he was helpless.

Hans Brock, one of the mates, died on 23 January after an illness that had lasted five months and had confined him to his bed for much of that

26

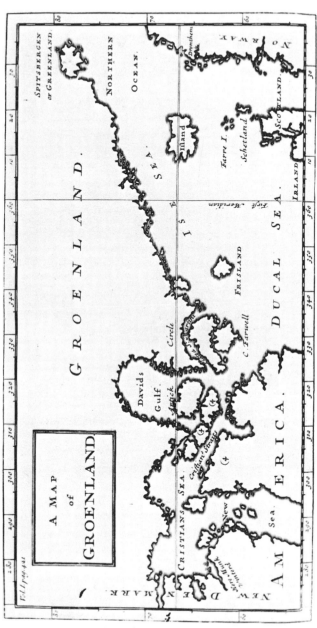

From Churchill's *Voyages*: London, 1732. ("A Collection of Voyages and Travels, Some Now First Printed from Original Manuscripts, Others Now First Published in English . . .") Photo courtesy of T. Fisher Rare Book Library.

time. On the same day the priest sat up in his berth and preached a sermon, the last one he was ever to deliver in this world.

On 24 January there appeared to be two suns in the sky.

When I had the body of Hans Brock buried on the twenty-fifth, I ordered that two falconets should be fired in his honour—the last honour that I could show him at our wintering place. But the very sharp frost had made the iron so brittle that the trunnions broke off both weapons when they were discharged, with the result that the man who fired them nearly lost his legs. One of the seamen, Jens Helsing, died two days later, and on the same day my lieutenant, the well-born Mauritz Stygge, took to his bed for the last time after a long illness. On that day, too, some of the men saw the tracks of five reindeer that were being pursued by a wolf. I sent a few men out to follow them, hoping to obtain some fresh meat, but a heavy fall of snow wiped out their tracks, and the men returned empty-handed.

On the night of the twenty-eighth the cold was so severe that it burst a tin kettle which the boy had left in the cabin with a little water in it. As tin cannot stand the terrible frosts of such icy seas, I don't know what kind of vessels should be used to preserve precious waters in that region. On 2 February the frost was still very sharp, but the men who were on shore got two ptarmigan, which served to refresh the men who were ill.

When Laurids Bergen, one of the seamen, died on 5 February, I sent an urgent message to the surgeon requesting, in God's name, that he assist us with whatever medicine or good advice he might have to offer. Because he himself was very ill and weak at the time, I suggested that he might like to tell me what medicine or remedy could be used for the benefit of the crew. And again he replied, as he had earlier, that without the assistance of God he was helpless.

On 6 February I went to the mouth of the river with three men to find out how matters stood with the ice at sea. As no open water was visible, we returned to the ship that evening. During the next few days the weather was rather mild, but the crew was still plagued with sickness and weakness. Two of the men died on the tenth, after having been ill for a very long time. We caught two ptarmigan on 12 February, which was a great consolation to the sick; and the next day I increased the rations so that each man received a third of a pint of wine daily and a full measure of spirits every morning in addition to his usual allowance.

During the next few days the number of sick men increased steadily. By the sixteenth there were only seven of us left who were healthy enough to fetch wood and water and to do whatever else had to be done on board. On that same day one of the seamen died—a man who had been ill for the whole voyage and who was as dirty as an untamed beast in his habits. Another man, Rasmus Kiöbenhauffn, died on the seventeenth, bringing the number who had already perished to twenty. On that day we got a hare, which was very welcome.

On 20 February the priest, Mr. Rasmus Jensen, died in the evening, after a long illness that had confined him to his bed for much of the time. Very little happened during the following days except the death of Claus, the lieutenant's servant, who had long been ill. Then, on the night of 25 February, a kettle that was used for melting snow was burst by the frost when a little water was left in the bottom. On 29 February the frost was so severe that no one could go ashore to fetch wood or water, so that the cook was forced to use whatever he could find on board for fuel. Towards evening, however, I did manage to get some wood hauled aboard. In order to get something to eat that day, I was obliged to tend the cabin myself, because my servant had also fallen ill by that time and had taken to his bed.

Jens Borringholm and Hans Skudenes died on 1 March. As nearly all the crew were sick by that time, we were having great difficulty in burying the dead.

The weather during most of March was mild. On the fourth we caught five ptarmigan, which were a welcome addition to our diet. The men could not eat the meat because their mouths were so swollen and inflamed with scurvy, but they drank the broth that was distributed amongst them. After an illness that lasted almost nine weeks, Oluf Boye died on 8 March and was immediately buried. Anders, the cooper, died on the ninth, having been ill since Christmas; he too was buried the following day.

The sun entered the constellation Aries on 11 March, marking the vernal equinox, when day and night are of equal length. In that latitude the sun rose in the east-southeast, and set in the west-northwest at seven o'clock in the evening. Actually, it was not more than six o'clock, because of the variation. Because the day was fine and mild, I had all the snow shovelled off the deck and generally cleaned up the ship. At the time, there were very few of the men who could still do any work. Around 21 March the weather was changeable, with some days mild and clear and others cold and stormy. Most of the crew were so sick that they were both melancholy to listen to and miserable to behold. Mr. Casper, the surgeon, died that same day, as did Povel Pedersen; both of them had been ill most of the time since Christmas. By the time they died, the illness was raging more violently amongst the crew each day, so that most of those who were still alive were too sick even to bury the dead.

Around 24 March it was mild and clear without a trace of frost, so that we were led to hope that the weather might finally become more favourable. When one of the men went ashore and climbed a high rock, he saw open water outside the harbour, a sight which filled us with confidence. Then, after being sick in bed for nineteen weeks, the skipper of the *Unicorn*, Jan Ollufsen, died the next day. As the weather was very good that day, I went ashore myself and collected *tydebaer* (as they are called in Norway) in places where the snow had already melted. Oddly enough, they were just as fresh as they had been in the fall, although they had to be picked immediately because they withered so quickly. As the weather continued to be good, I went ashore again the next day to collect berries. I distributed them among the men, who found them both tasty and agreeable.

On 27 March I opened the surgeon's chest to examine its contents in detail, for as we no longer had a surgeon, I had to do whatever I could myself. And then I discovered what a serious oversight had been made in not providing a list that would tell us what the medicines were good for, and how they were to be used. I would also stake my life on the opinion that even the surgeon did not know how those medicines were to be used, for all the labels were written in Latin, and whenever he wished to read one, he had to call the priest to translate it for him.

The weather continued to be rather mild till 29 March, when Ismael Abrahamsen and Christen Gregersen died. They were buried that same day, as we had both the opportunity and the ability at that time. Suend Arffuedsen, one of the carpenters, died on 30 March during a very sharp frost. My greatest sorrow and misery started at that time, and soon I was like a wild and lonely bird. I was obliged to prepare and serve drink to the sick men myself, and to give them anything else I thought might nourish or comfort them. I was not accustomed to such duties, however, and had but little knowledge of what should be done. Johan Petterson, my second mate, died on 31 March, after a long illness during which he was confined to his bed, and my nephew, Erich Munk, died the following day. Both bodies were placed together in a single grave.

On 3 April there was such a fearfully sharp frost that none of us could get out of bed; nor did I have any men left to command, for they were all lying under the hand of God. Amidst all that misery and sorrow, Iffuer

Alsing died. Next day the weather was so bitterly cold that it was impossible for anyone to dig a grave to bury the dead bodies that were in the ship. Then, on the fifth, Christoffer Opslöe and Rasmus Clemendsen, my chief gunner and mate, both died; and later that same day Lauritz Hansen also died. By that time the number of healthy men was so small that we could scarcely muster a burial party.

On 8 April William Gordon, my chief mate, died after a long illness; and that evening Anders Sodens also died. We buried them, too, in a common grave. We who were still alive managed to bury them, but only with great difficulty because of the miserable weakness that was upon us. We were so weak that not one of us was able to fetch wood from the forest. For fuel, we were forced to break up anything in the ship that would burn, even our own shallop.

On 10 April, after a long illness, the honourable and well-born Mauritz Stygge died. Because he was my lieutenant, I wrapped his body in some of my own linen as well as I could. A coffin was made for him, but only with great difficulty. The twelfth of April was a fine day, with some sunshine and the first rain we had seen for seven months. We carried the lieutenant's body ashore, where we buried it with such propriety as the time and place afforded.

On 13 April I took a bath in a wine cask. I added to the water some of each of the different herbs that we found in the medicine chest and that we thought might be helpful. After me, those men who still had the strength to move about also took a bath. Thanks be to God, that bath did us much good, me in particular. The next day there was a sharp frost, and only four men besides myself were strong enough to sit up in their berths to hear the homily for Good Friday. Anders Oroust and Jens, the cooper, died on Easter Day, 16 April, after a long illness; and as the weather was fairly mild, we managed to bury them that same day. Although he was ill himself, I immediately promoted my quartermaster to the position of master so that he might assist me with whatever strength he could still muster. For by that time I too was quite miserable and felt abandoned by the entire world, as you may imagine. During the following night Hans Bendtsen died, and on the seventeenth my servant, Olluff Andersen, who had served me well and faithfully for seven years, also died. Peder Amundsen died on 19 April. He had been ill for a long time and was quite wasted away by the disease. On 20 April, a fine sunny day with an east wind, we got three ptarmigan.

When the fine weather continued the next day, some of the sick men

A map from Jens Munk's original journal. An unusual feature of this map is that south is represented by the top of the map and north by the bottom. Thus Munk's wintering place is seen on the extreme right. From *Danish Arctic Expeditions, 1605-1620*, ed. C.C.A. Gosch. Courtesy of the Hakluyt Society.

crawled out of their berths to warm themselves in the sun. But they were so weak that many of them fainted, and we found it almost impossible to get them back into bed. That same evening we got two grouse, which again provided some fresh meat for the comfort of the sick. This was due to God's special providence, for the sick could no longer eat any of the salted meat but only the broth of such fresh meat as we could obtain.

During the afternoon of 22 April all of us who were strong enough had a bath, which we again found very refreshing. Alluff Sundmöer, who was mate to the quartermaster, died on 24 April. Then, on the twenty-fifth, we were delighted to see that the wild geese were returning. We hoped that this would announce the arrival of summer, but it was not to be, for the cold weather continued.

On the night of 27 April there was a sharp frost and a south wind, which was an unusual combination. Because of our weakened condition, we felt the cold more acutely than we had previously, and it caused us much distress. Halffword Bronnie died on that same day, after an illness which lasted more than two months. We had great difficulty in getting him buried. The next day Thoer Thonsberg and Morton Nielsen, my butler, both died; and by that time, although there were only four of us left who were able to move about, we did manage to bury them. On 3 and 4 May not a man was able to leave his berth except for the assistant cook and myself; and on the fourth both Anders Marstrand and Morten Marstrand, a boatswain's mate, died after a long illness. On the sixth, John Watson, the English pilot, died. The bodies of these last three men were left lying in their berths because the weather was so bad, and there were now only three of us left who had strength enough to move around. We finally managed to bury them on 7 May, when the weather became milder. By that time, however, we were so weak that we could no longer carry the dead bodies to their graves but had to drag them there on the small sled that was used for hauling wood.

Although the weather was still very cold on the tenth, it was also clear, and great numbers of geese arrived from the south. We managed to get one of them, which lasted for two meals. At that time there were eleven of us still alive, including the sick and the dying. The eleventh was again so bitterly cold that we all stayed quietly in our berths, for by that time we were so extremely weak that the cold seemed to crush and paralyze our limbs. The next day Suend Marstrand and Jens Jörgensen, one of the carpenters, both died, and only God can know the torments we suffered before we got them to their graves. Those were the last bodies that we buried.

On 16 May, when it was particularly cold, the skipper of the *Lamprey*, Jens Hendrichsen, died. His was the first body that had to remain unburied.

Erich Hansen died on 19 May. Throughout the entire voyage he had been industrious and congenial and had neither offended anyone nor merited any punishment. He had dug many graves for others, but now that there was no one left who could dig a grave for him, his own body was left unburied. The following day was mild and sunny, with the wind from the south. It was a great sorrow to us that now, when God had sent us such an abundance of different kinds of fowl, none of us was strong enough to go hunting.

As the twenty-first was again clear and sunny, I and three of the men went ashore, where we built a fire and anointed our joints with bear grease. In the evening I returned on board with one of the men, leaving the other two on shore. On 22 May God sent us a day that was as fine and sunny as could be wished for; and by Divine Providence a goose approached the ship that day—a goose that had had one of its legs shot off a few days before. We shot the bird, and it supplied us with broth for two days. A wide variety of birds had arrived in the country during the previous week. There were several different kinds of geese and swans, a variety of ducks, as well as terns, southern pewits, swallows, snipe (a very toothsome bird), gulls, falcons, ravens, ptarmigan, and eagles.

During the next few days there was nothing in particular to write about. There were only seven of us miserable people still alive, and we lay there day after day looking mournfully at each other, hoping that the snow would melt and that the ice would drift away. The illness that had fallen upon us was rare and extraordinary, with most peculiar symptoms. The limbs and joints were miserably drawn together, and there were great pains in the loins as if a thousand knives had been thrust there. At the same time the body was discoloured as when someone has a black eye, and all the limbs were powerless. The mouth, too, was in a miserable condition, as all the teeth were loose, so that it was impossible to eat.

Then, while we were lying helplessly in bed, Peder Nyborg, one of the carpenters, Knud Lauritzsen Skudenes, and Jorgen, the cook's boy, all died. Their bodies were simply left in the steerage, for there was no one left who had the strength to bury them or even to throw them overboard.

By 4 June there were only four of us left alive, and we just lay there unable to do a thing. Our appetites and digestions were sound, but our teeth were so loose that we could not eat; nor did we have the strength to go down to the hold for more wine. The cook's boy lay dead beside my berth, while three others lay dead in the steerage. Two men were still on shore, simply because they were too weak from the illness to climb back on board. And in addition, none of us had had any sustenance for four days. I could hope for nothing, under the circumstances, but that God would put an end to my misery by taking me to Himself and His Kingdom; and so, believing it would be the last thing I would ever write in this world, I penned the following:

> Inasmuch as I have no more hope of life in this world, I request (for the sake of God) that if any Christians should happen to come this way, they bury my poor body in the earth, together with the others that are lying here. Their reward they may expect from God. I request further that this, my journal, may be sent to my most gracious Lord and King (for every word that is found herein is true) in order that my poor wife and children may obtain some benefit from my great distress and miserable death. Herewith, goodnight to all the world; and my soul into the hands of God, etc.,

> Jens Munk

On 8 June, as I could no longer stand the smell of the dead bodies that had remained on the ship so long, I managed to crawl out of my berth. For surely it would not matter where I died—whether I perished in my berth or outside among the others who were lying there dead. When I came out of my cabin—with the assistance of God—I spent the night on deck, wrapped in the clothing of those who were already dead. The next day, to my astonishment, I saw the two men who were still on shore. I thought they too had died long ago. When they saw me, they came out on the ice to the ship to help me get ashore and to gather up the clothes which I threw overboard. Fortunately, the ship was no more than 12 or 14 fathom from shore. For some time after that we dwelt under a bush on shore, where we built a fire each day. Later on we were able to crawl around looking for any green thing that grew out of the earth. Whenever we found something, we would dig it up and suck the juice out of its main root. This we found very helpful; and as the heat of the sun grew stronger each day, we slowly began to recover. But the sailmaker, meanwhile, had died on the ship.

When the ice began drifting away about 18 June, we got a flounder-net out of the sloop and set it at low tide. With the returning flood God sent us six large trout which I cooked myself, while the two others went aboard the *Lamprey* to fetch wine. That, incidentally, was the first wine we had tasted for some time, as we had lost our appetite for it. In the days that followed we got fresh fish every day, and although we could not eat the flesh, we drank the broth with wine. And so, by degrees, we recovered. We even brought a gun ashore to shoot birds, which we also found very refreshing.

After we had asked Our Lord for counsel and good fortune, we set to work on 26 June, in the name of Jesus, to bring the *Lamprey* alongside the *Unicorn* and worked as diligently as we could in preparing her sails. We encountered great difficulties in this and suffered much anxiety, because the *Lamprey* stood high and dry on shore, having been carried there by the winter flood. We were obliged, therefore, to unload her completely and then wait for a high spring tide to float her off; but we were finally successful. When we climbed aboard the *Unicorn*, our first job was to throw the decomposed bodies overboard because the smell was so bad that we couldn't stand it. Yet the three of us had to get all our food and drink from that ship, as well as everything else we would need for crossing the ocean sea, for there was none other to be had.

At that time it was as warm there as it might have been in Denmark, with the cloudberries already in bud and at least one shower of rain each day. There was also such a quantity of gnats that they were unbearable in calm weather. Before leaving, I drilled two or three holes in the hull of the *Unicorn* so that she would always fill with water at high tide, and thus the weight of the water would keep her firmly bedded down when the tide was out. The harbour where we had spent the winter I named "Jens Munk's Bay". And finally, on the afternoon of Sunday, 16 July, we set sail, in the name of God, from our harbour.

Late the next afternoon we encountered a lot of ice and were forced to stand off and on. During the night, however, the weather became calm and misty, and we found ourselves stuck firmly in the ice. As a result, I had to abandon the *Unicorn*'s boat; we had taken it in tow, hoping to use it when we wanted to go ashore. On the twentieth a great white bear approached the ship while we were drifting helplessly with the ice. As soon as he saw us he turned and ran, followed by a large dog that we had aboard. Although the dog never returned to the ship, we could still hear him howling two days later.

On 22 July there was a heavy gale which pounded us incessantly against the ice. Each time we struck, it was like striking a rock, and finally our rudder was damaged. I managed to turn the ship by throwing a grapnel onto a large slab of ice, and this saved us from being swept to destruction. We continued thus to drift with the ice through 24 and 25 July. When we finally got clear of the ice on 26 July, I turned to the east, trying to feel my way between the ice and the southern shore. We sailed into 38 fathom (with a sandy bottom) and then kept beating back and forth but were unable to find a path that way. The following afternoon we saw the ship's boat that we had set adrift ten days before. On 28 July I spent all day tacking back and forth between the shore and the ice before I came to the conclusion that there was no hope of getting around the ice by the southeast.

The following morning I stood again to the northwest. I became trapped in the ice once more on 30 July, when the fog became so thick that we could not exercise sufficient vigilance. But we worked our way out of the ice the next day and shaped our course northwest till the wind became so high that I took in the foresail and let the sloop drift under her course alone. By 4 August I was once more sailing north between the ice and the western shore of Hudson Bay. But the next night the ice came so strongly against me that I was obliged to come into 12 fathom before I could double around it. It should be noted, incidentally, that the ice in that area drifts to the south, following the shore. When I came into 45 fathom on 6 August, I shaped my course to the east-northeast, without observing any more ice.

On 8 August I sailed 187 miles in 24 hours, east-northeast, and on the ninth I had sailed 178 miles on the same course when the wind shifted to the east, bringing a sharp frost. The following day was cold and foggy, with a heavy gale from the east which forced us to lay to. On 11 August, with the weather somewhat unsettled but with the wind mainly from the east, I stood to the north and picked up Carys Swan Nest with the dawn, at $62\frac{1}{2}°$ north. Staying about five miles off shore, I followed the coastline of that flat, barren land, steering east-northeast, over a hard, stony bottom in 40 fathom. I continued sailing east-northeast on 12 August, pushed along by a light breeze. Early the next morning I picked up the northeast point of Mansel Island, where we encountered a lot of ice along the shore. Towards the south, particularly, the island is low and flat; the eastern point is located at 63° north. Because the ice was so thick in the area, we were forced to stand off and on for 24 hours.

14 August 1620

On the morning of 14 August, I found myself in a narrow channel where I was heavily beset with ice on all sides; so I took in the mainsail and worked my way through the ice with the foresail alone, till I reached open water around noon. As I shaped my course east-southeast, I had Salisbury and Nottingham Islands to port and Digges Islands close under the mainland to starboard. At that point I was leaving Hudson Bay and entering Hudson Strait. The next day we encountered a fair amount of ice, but continued to "luff on" and "hold firm the grapnel". A lot of snow fell that day, and the wild geese were already flying south.

Finding myself close to the northern shore of the strait on 16 August, I shaped my course southeast by east, true. When the wind shifted to the northwest the next day, I changed my course to southeast. That night was cold and foggy, but it cleared up by noon the next day, and by that evening we picked up Hatton Headland at the southern tip of Resolution Island. From this cape the coast trends northerly towards Davis Strait on one side and northwestward into Hudson Strait on the other.

On 19 August we had a strong west wind and thick weather, during which we passed a number of scattered icebergs. That day we sailed 187 miles in 24 hours. The next day we sailed 140 miles before a moderate breeze. All that night we had rain and a northeast wind. In the morning it settled down to a stiff gale, so that we sailed about 94 miles in those 24 hours. During the next 24 hours, with a stiff breeze, we sailed 165 miles under our mainsail alone. On 23 August we sailed 126 miles; our latitude at noon was 58°44' north. That evening the wind fell off, which was rather fortunate, because we had to do some work on the pump, which was not operating properly. On the twenty-fourth we had a gale from the east, so we sailed about 95 miles to the south-southeast, then swung around to the north at noon. Then for the next three days we had a dead calm.

A good brisk wind from the northwest returned on the twenty-ninth, so we shaped our course east by north, but the wind soon shifted to the north and increased to a gale, forcing us to lie a-hull and man the pumps. It was not till the thirty-first that we could set any sail, and then only the small mainsail, because the weather was still heavy. For the next three days, the wind raged out of the southeast with enough violence to sweep a man off his feet. Towards evening we were forced to take in all the sails and lie a-hull while we worked the pumps. On 4 September we had very heavy rain with a small gale, so that we were not able to leave the pumps. Towards evening, when the wind dropped off a little, we finally got some rest. We simply let the sloop drift through the night under bare poles—so far as the pump would let us—for we were thoroughly exhausted.

At noon the next day I observed the sun and found that our latitude was 58°59' north; the wind was easterly, with rain and a somewhat rough sea. That night the wind was very moderate, and in the morning it died down even further. The next day, the seventh, we were at 59°15' north, with a nice moderate breeze, so we triced up the tack, just as the wind fell off again. On the eighth our latitude was 60°19' north, with a light westerly wind. For the next three days we had a variety of winds and a great deal of fog. About dusk on 11 September we were hit by a gale which tore our foresail out of its boltropes, and by the time the three of us managed to take it in, the sloop was half full of water.

On the night of the twelfth the wind shifted to the west, where it blew so hard that it parted our topsail sheet and broke both the topmast stay and the great parrel. The next day, when I thought we were about the same longitude as the Shetland Islands, we sighted a ship. Twice, we managed to get close enough to speak to the people on board, but she was unable to assist us because the wind was too high.

We raised the Orkney Islands on 14 September and passed them the following day with the wind at the southeast. Steering east by north towards Norway, we sailed 95 miles on 16 September. We continued on the same course through the next day, but shifted it a bit to the south at ten o'clock on the morning of the eighteenth. Then, after lying a-hull all through the nineteenth because of a gale, we finally sighted Norway on 20 September.

The next day we entered a harbour south of Aldon in a flying gale, not knowing where we were. Although we found ourselves in a large fjord protected by some rocky islands, I spent the rest of the day beating back and forth, because I had only half an anchor. Late in the afternoon, when I saw that no one was coming out to assist us, I ran the sloop into a small bay and dropped my broken anchor. Because I had no boat to carry a hawser ashore, I had to lie there without being moored. That evening a peasant happened to wander by, but before he would assist me in getting a hawser ashore, I had to threaten him with a gun. In the morning I proceeded in the peasant's boat to His Majesty's bailiff in Söndfjord and asked him to send fresh food and men aboard the sloop so that it could be taken to Bergen. Then, with the ship properly looked after and ourselves in a Christian country once again, our joy was so great we could not hold back our tears, and we thanked God that He had graciously granted us such happiness.

On 25 September I arrived at Bergen, where I went immediately to a physician to obtain advice and remedies. I also arranged for drinks and medicine to be taken to my two men by the skipper who was to replace me on the *Lamprey*. Then, on 27 September 1620, I wrote to the high authorities in Denmark to report that I was home.